U.S. Sites and Symbols

★★★★★★★★★★★★★

Flowers

Leia Tait

WEIGL PUBLISHERS INC.

Published by Weigl Publishers Inc.
350 5th Avenue, Suite 3304, PMB 6G
New York, NY 10118-0069

Website: www.weigl.com

All of the Internet URLs given in the book were valid at the time of publication. However, due to the dynamic nature of the Internet, some addresses may have changed, or sites may have ceased to exist since publication. While the author and publisher regret any inconvenience this may cause readers, no responsibility for any such changes can be accepted by either the author or the publisher.

Tait, Leia.
Flowers / Leia Tait.
          p. cm. – (U.S. sites and symbols)
Includes index.
ISBN: 978-1-59036-895-4 (soft cover: alk. Paper) – ISBN: 978-1-59036-894-7 (hard cover: alk. Paper) 1. State flowers—United States—Juvenile literature. I. Title.
QK85.T352009
582.130973—DC22

2008015827

Printed in the United States of America
1 2 3 4 5 6 7 8 9 0 12 11 10 09 08

Editor: Danielle LeClair
Designer: Kathryn Livingstone

Photograph Credits

Weigl acknowledges Shutterstock, iStockphoto, and Dreamstime as the primary image suppliers for this title. Unless otherwise noted, all images herein were obtained from Shutterstock, iStockphoto, Dreamstime and their contributors.

Other photograph credits include: Alamy: pages, 14 (middle and bottom), 20 (top, in box), 28 (top, bottom box), 30 (top, behind), 35 (top); Photo by R.L. Ash: page 31 (bottom).

Every reasonable effort has been made to trace ownership and to obtain permission to reprint copyright material. The publishers would be pleased to have any errors or omissions brought to their attention so that they may be corrected in subsequent printings.

Contents

What are Symbols?

A symbol is an item that stands for something else. Objects, artworks, or living things can all be symbols. Every U.S. state has official symbols, or emblems. These items represent the people, history, and culture of the state. State symbols create feelings of pride and **citizenship** among the people who live there. Each of the 50 U.S. states has an official flower. It is called the state flower or the floral emblem.

State Flower

The idea of state flowers start[ed in]
1893. That year, a huge fair was
held in Chicago, Illinois. The fair
was called the World's Columbian
Exposition. Countries from
around the world made displays
for the fair. Women who helped
plan the fair's U.S. displays asked
each state to choose a flower to
represent it. The women used the
flowers to make a special exhibit.
It was called the "National
Garland of Flowers." Most states
still use the state flower they
chose for the national garland
in 1893.

The World's Columbian Exposition
lasted an entire year. More than 21
million people attended.

Alaska

Hawai'i

Washington

Montana

Oregon

Idaho

Wyoming

The West

Nevada

Utah

Colorado

California

Arizona

New Mexico

Each state has a flower symbol. In this book, the states are organized by region. These regions are the West, the Midwest, the South, and the Northeast. Each region is unique because of its land, people, and wildlife. Throughout this book, the regions are color coded. To find a state flower, first find the state using the map on this page. Then, turn to the pages that are the same color as that state.

The Northeast

New Hampshire
Vermont
Massachusetts
Maine
New York
Rhode Island
Connecticut
New Jersey
Delaware
Maryland
Pennsylvania

North Dakota
Minnesota
South Dakota
Iowa
Nebraska
Kansas

The Midwest

Wisconsin
Michigan
Ohio
Indiana
Illinois
Missouri

West Virginia
Virginia
Kentucky
North Carolina
Tennessee
South Carolina

The South

Oklahoma
Arkansas
Texas
Louisiana
Mississippi
Alabama
Georgia
Florida

Web Crawler

Find out facts about each state at
www.americaslibrary.gov. Click on
"Explore the States."

The West

The West is made up of 13 states. They are Alaska, Arizona, California, Colorado, Hawai'i, Idaho, Montana, Nevada, New Mexico, Oregon, Utah, Washington, and Wyoming. Alaska is far to the north. It is separated from the rest of the country by Canada. The Pacific Ocean borders Alaska, Washington, Oregon, and California, and surrounds Hawai'i.

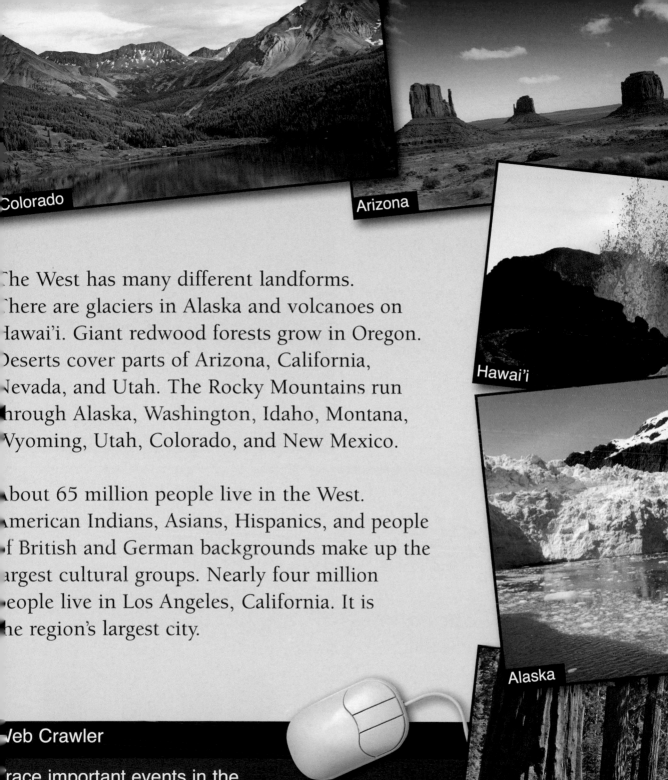

Colorado

Arizona

Hawai'i

Alaska

California

The West has many different landforms. There are glaciers in Alaska and volcanoes on Hawai'i. Giant redwood forests grow in Oregon. Deserts cover parts of Arizona, California, Nevada, and Utah. The Rocky Mountains run through Alaska, Washington, Idaho, Montana, Wyoming, Utah, Colorado, and New Mexico.

About 65 million people live in the West. American Indians, Asians, Hispanics, and people of British and German backgrounds make up the largest cultural groups. Nearly four million people live in Los Angeles, California. It is the region's largest city.

Web Crawler

Trace important events in the history of the West at **www.pbs.org/ weta/thewest/events**.

Discover the West's natural wonders by clicking on the states at **www.nps.gov**.

Alaska
Forget-Me-Not

Alaska's state flower is the forget-me-not. This is a type of wildflower. The forget-me-not has five sky-blue petals with a white ring around a yellow center. The forget-me-not blooms during the summer. It has been Alaska's official flower since 1917.

Arizona
Saguaro Cactus Blossom

Arizona chose the saguaro cactus blossom as its state flower in 1931. The saguaro cactus is the biggest cactus in the United States. It can grow up to 40 feet tall. Saguaro cactus blossoms are white with yellow centers. They open at night and stay open for only one day. After they close, the flowers change into red fruit. The fruit can be eaten raw or made into jam.

California
Golden Poppy

The golden poppy became the state flower of California in 1903. In early spring, thousands of these flowers cover California's hills. Golden poppies have silky, fan-shaped petals. They are usually orange but can also be yellow, peach, red, or pink. Golden poppies are sometimes called the *copa de oro*. This means "cup of gold" in Spanish.

Colorado
White and Lavender Columbine

Colorado's state flower is the white and lavender columbine. This wildflower often grows at the bottom of mountains. The white and lavender columbine is

sometimes called the Rocky Mountain columbine or the Colorado columbine. It became Colorado's state flower in 1899. Today, this flower is rare in nature. In Colorado, it is illegal to uproot the plant or pick more than 25 of the flowers in one day.

Hawai'i
Yellow Hibiscus

The hibiscus flower is the symbol of Hawai'i. Yellow hibiscus became Hawai'i's state flower in 1988. The yellow hibiscus is a tropical flower that grows naturally on six out of eight of the main islands. Once, yellow hibiscus grew on all of the Hawai'ian Islands. Today, it is **endangered**. Only about 60 yellow hibiscus plants still live in nature.

Idaho
Syringa

Idaho's state flower is the syringa. It became the state flower in 1931. The syringa is a white flower with four petals. It grows in clusters on leafy shrubs. Syringas grow naturally in the western states. They are often called the mockorange because they smell like orange blossoms.

Montana
Bitterroot

Bitterroot is the state flower of Montana. It is a pink wildflower. In the past, American Indian groups used the plant's roots for food. The first Europeans to learn about bitterroot were explorers Meriwether Lewis and William Clark. They wrote about all its uses in 1805. Bitterroot became Montana's state flower 90 years later, in 1895.

Nevada
Sagebrush

In 1917, the government of Nevada chose sagebrush as its state emblem. Over time, Nevada adopted more symbols. Sagebrush became the state's

official flower in 1956. This gray-green plant has small, pale yellow flowers. Sagebrush grows naturally throughout the West. It is well known for its pleasant smell.

New Mexico
Yucca

The yucca became New Mexico's state flower in 1927. Yuccas are a type of lily. They grow naturally in the deserts of the West. The yucca plant is also sometimes called the soapweed. In the past, American Indians made soap from the plant's roots.

Oregon
Oregon Grape

The Oregon grape has been Oregon's state flower since 1899. The Oregon grape grows along the Pacific coast. It has thick, shiny leaves and dark blue berries. Its small, delicate flowers bloom in early summer.

Utah
Sego Lily

In 1911, Utah's schoolchildren chose the sego lily for the state flower. This tulip-like flower has three petals and grows in Utah's grasslands. Sego lilies can be white, lilac, or yellow in color. During the mid-1800s, food was scarce in Utah. Settlers survived by eating the roots of sego lilies.

Washington
Coast Rhododendron

Washington's state flower is the coast rhododendron. It was chosen by the women of Washington in 1892. Coast rhododendrons are pink, bell-shaped flowers that are **evergreen** plants. They have five wavy petals. Bunches of 20 or more of these flowers grow together in round clusters.

Wyoming
Indian Paintbrush

The Indian paintbrush became Wyoming's state flower in 1917. It is a type of wildflower. Indian paintbrush flowers are small. They are hidden by spiky, red-tipped **sepals**. The sepals are often mistaken for the flower. They look like a brush that has been dipped in paint. Indian paintbrushes are sometimes also called painted cups or desert paintbrushes.

The Midwest

The Midwest is in the center of the United States. It lies between the Rocky Mountains in the west and the Appalachian Mountains in the northeast. The Ohio River separates the Midwest from the South. Canada lies to the north. There are 12 states in the Midwest. They are Illinois, Indiana, Iowa, Kansas, Michigan, Minnesota, Missouri, Nebraska, North Dakota, Ohio, South Dakota, and Wisconsin.

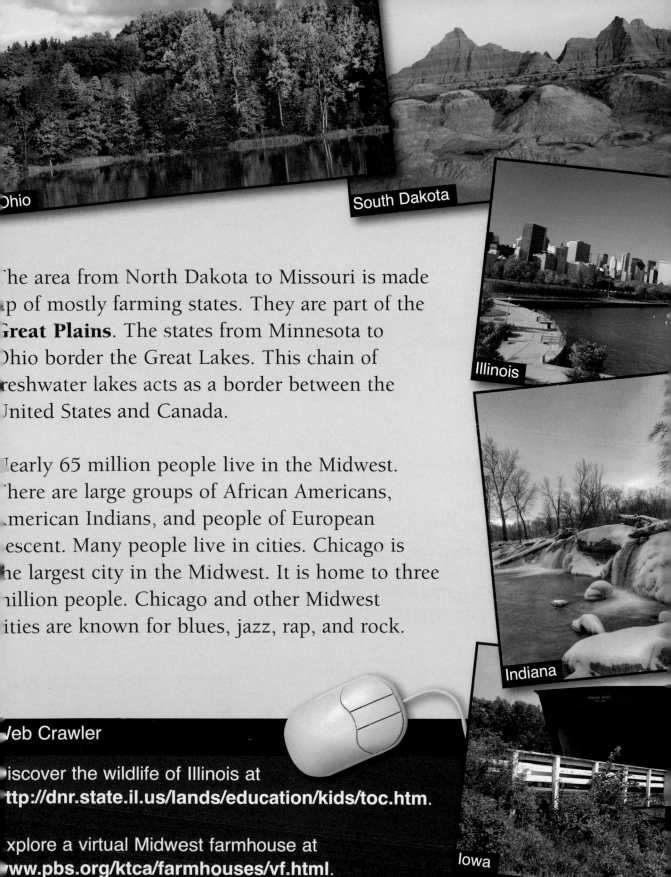

Ohio

South Dakota

Illinois

The area from North Dakota to Missouri is made up of mostly farming states. They are part of the **Great Plains**. The states from Minnesota to Ohio border the Great Lakes. This chain of freshwater lakes acts as a border between the United States and Canada.

Nearly 65 million people live in the Midwest. There are large groups of African Americans, American Indians, and people of European descent. Many people live in cities. Chicago is the largest city in the Midwest. It is home to three million people. Chicago and other Midwest cities are known for blues, jazz, rap, and rock.

Indiana

Web Crawler

Discover the wildlife of Illinois at
http://dnr.state.il.us/lands/education/kids/toc.htm.

Explore a virtual Midwest farmhouse at
www.pbs.org/ktca/farmhouses/vf.html.

Iowa

Illinois
Blue Violet

In 1908, the Illinois government made the blue violet the state's official flower. Blue violets are common wildflowers, and there are eight types in Illinois. One type is the dooryard violet. The dooryard violet is most often used as Illinois' floral emblem. It has purplish-blue flowers that bloom in spring.

Indiana
Peony

Indiana has changed its official flower four times. In 1913, the carnation became Indiana's first state flower. It was replaced by the blossom of the tulip tree in 1923 and the zinnia in 1931. In 1957, the peony became Indiana's new state flower. Peonies come from parts of Europe and China. They are large red, pink, or white flowers that have a strong smell. Peonies do not grow naturally in the United States but can be grown in gardens.

Iowa
Wild Rose

Iowa's state flower is the wild rose. It was chosen in 1897. Wild roses grow naturally throughout Iowa. They come in many shades of pink and have yellow centers. There are different types of wild roses. The wild prairie rose is usually used as Iowa's state flower.

Kansas
Sunflower

Kansas is often called "the sunflower state." The sunflower has grown in Kansas for thousands of years. It has been the state's official flower since 1903. Sunflowers can grow up to 12 feet tall. The flower head is made of many dark flowers clustered into a disc. Bright **ray flowers** circle the disc. The ray flowers are usually yellow, orange, or red. Sunflowers are named for the way they turn their head to follow the Sun.

Michigan
Apple Blossom & Dwarf Lake Iris

Michigan has two official flowers. They are the apple blossom and the dwarf lake iris. The apple blossom was chosen as Michigan's state flower in 1897. More than 20 different kinds of apple blossoms grow in Michigan. The dwarf lake iris is Michigan's official wildflower. It was chosen in 1997. The dwarf lake iris is found only near the Great Lakes.

Minnesota
Pink-and-White Lady's Slipper

Minnesota's state flower is the pink-and-white lady's slipper. This is a type of orchid. It became the state flower in 1902. The pink-and-white lady's slipper grows naturally in Minnesota and can live for 50 years. These flowers are rare. It is illegal in Minnesota to pick pink-and-white lady's slippers or uproot the plants.

Missouri
Hawthorn Blossom

Missouri chose the hawthorn blossom as its state flower in 1923. The hawthorn blossom is a white flower with a yellow-green center. It grows in clusters on hawthorn trees. There are many different types of hawthorn. More than 75 types are found in Missouri.

Nebraska
Goldenrod

Goldenrod became Nebraska's state flower in 1895. It is an **herb** that grows naturally in Nebraska. Goldenrod flowers are small and yellow and grow in clusters. It is a common floral symbol. Nebraska, Kentucky, and South Carolina all use goldenrod as the state flower.

North Dakota
Wild Prairie Rose

North Dakota's state flower is the wild prairie rose. The state government adopted the flower in 1907. The wild prairie rose has five bright pink petals and a yellow center. It grows naturally in meadows throughout North Dakota.

Ohio
Scarlet Carnation & White Trillium

The scarlet carnation is from Europe. President William McKinley, who was from Ohio, often wore a scarlet carnation in his buttonhole. In memory of McKinley, the Ohio government chose the scarlet carnation as the state flower in 1904. In 1987, the white trillium became Ohio's state wildflower. It has three large white petals and three large leaves. *Trillium* is the Latin word for "three."

South Dakota
Pasque Flower

South Dakota's state flower is the pasque flower. It sometimes is called the May Day flower. The pasque is a small, light purple wildflower. It is one of the first flowers to bloom in spring. American Indians wrote many songs and stories about the pasque flower. It became South Dakota's state flower in 1903.

Wisconsin
Wood Violet

The wood violet is the state flower of Wisconsin. It was chosen by the state's schoolchildren in 1909.

This small wildflower has blue or purple petals and grows in South Dakota's woodlands and meadows. The flowers bloom in spring, and they can be eaten.

The South

The South is made up of 16 states. They are Alabama, Arkansas, Delaware, Florida, Georgia, Kentucky, Louisiana, Maryland, Mississippi, North Carolina, Oklahoma, South Carolina, Tennessee, Texas, Virginia, and West Virginia. The Atlantic Ocean borders the South from Delaware to the tip of Florida. A part of the Atlantic Ocean called the Gulf of Mexico stretches from Florida's west coast to Texas. Mexico lies to the south.

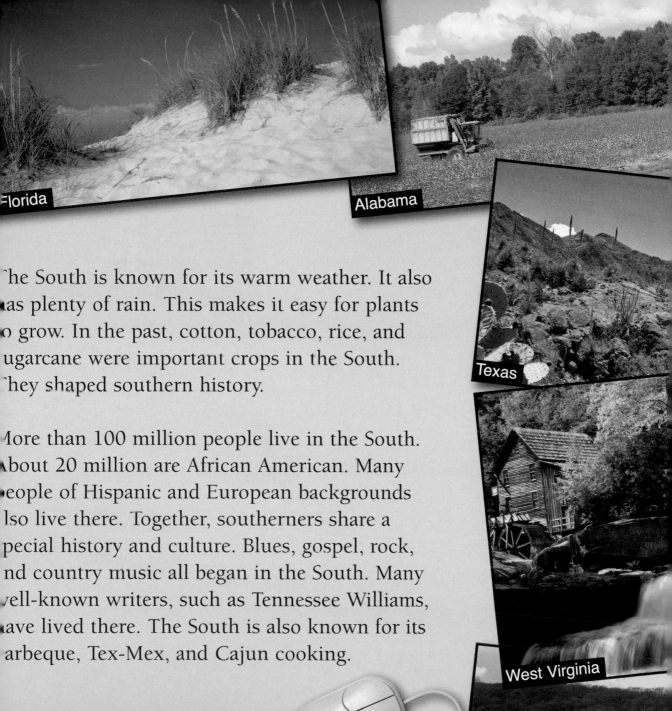

Florida

Alabama

Texas

West Virginia

Mississippi

The South is known for its warm weather. It also has plenty of rain. This makes it easy for plants to grow. In the past, cotton, tobacco, rice, and sugarcane were important crops in the South. They shaped southern history.

More than 100 million people live in the South. About 20 million are African American. Many people of Hispanic and European backgrounds also live there. Together, southerners share a special history and culture. Blues, gospel, rock, and country music all began in the South. Many well-known writers, such as Tennessee Williams, have lived there. The South is also known for its barbeque, Tex-Mex, and Cajun cooking.

Web Crawler

Read about the history of the South at **www.factmonster.com/ipka/A0875011.html**.

Explore the fun facts about the Southern States at **www.emints.org/ethemes/resources/00000575.shtml**.

Alabama
Camellia & Oak-leaf Hydrangea

The camellia became Alabama's state flower in 1959. Camellias come from Asia. In 1999, Alabama

chose the oak-leaf hydrangea as its state wildflower. This is a type of shrub with white flowers.

Arkansas
Apple Blossom

In 1901, Arkansas chose the apple blossom for its state flower. At the time, Arkansas grew many apples. Apple blossoms grow on apple trees and have five white-and-pink petals with green leaves.

Delaware
Peach Blossom

During the late 1800s, Delaware was known as "The Peach State." It had more than 800,000 peach trees. The peach blossom became Delaware's floral emblem in 1895. Peach blossoms come in many shades of pink.

Florida
Orange Blossom & Tickseed

Florida chose the orange blossom as its state flower in 1909. In spring, millions of these white flowers bloom on Florida orange trees. In 1991, the tickseed became Florida's state wildflower. Tickseed blossoms have yellow centers with yellow, pink, or white ray flowers.

Georgia
Cherokee Rose & Azalea

The Cherokee rose became Georgia's state flower in 1916. This is a white rose from Asia. Georgia's state wildflower is the azalea. It was chosen in 1979. These funnel-shaped flowers can be white, yellow, orange, red, or pink.

Kentucky
Goldenrod

Goldenrod became Kentucky's state flower in 1926. There are nearly 100 species of goldenrod, and 30 of them are found in Kentucky. Branches of goldenrod decorate the state flag.

Louisiana
Magnolia & Louisiana Iris

The magnolia has been Louisiana's state flower since 1900. Louisiana's state wildflower is the Louisiana iris. It was chosen in 1990. The Louisiana iris can be blue, purple, white, orange, or yellow. Magnolias are white flowers that grow on magnolia trees.

Maryland
Black-eyed Susan

In 1918, the black-eyed Susan became Maryland's state flower. This daisy has bright yellow petals around a dark brown center. Maryland's state bird, cat, flag, flower, and insect are also yellow and brown.

Mississippi
Magnolia

Mississippi schoolchildren chose the magnolia as the state flower in 1900. The state government approved this choice in 1952. The magnolia was named for the French botanist Pierre Magnol.

North Carolina
Dogwood Blossom

North Carolina's state flower is the dogwood blossom. It became the state flower in 1941. White or pink dogwood blossoms grow on dogwood trees.

Oklahoma
Mistletoe, Indian Blanket, & Oklahoma Rose

Oklahoma is the only state with three flower symbols. The first is mistletoe. Mistletoe grows on evergreen trees in Oklahoma. It became Oklahoma's state flower in 1910. That same year, the Indian blanket became the state wildflower. This is a red flower with yellow tips. It is sometimes called the firewheel. In 2004, the Oklahoma rose became Oklahoma's second state flower. This rose was first grown in 1964 at Oklahoma State University. It is dark red and has a sweet smell.

South Carolina
Yellow Jessamine & Tall Goldenrod

The yellow jessamine became South Carolina's state flower in 1924. Jessamine is a climbing plant. It climbs up trees and fences. Its yellow flowers are trumpet-shaped. In 2003, South Carolina chose tall goldenrod as the state wildflower. Tall goldenrod is a hardy plant, with long-lasting flowers.

Tennessee
Passionflower & Iris

Tennessee has two flower symbols. They are the passionflower and the iris. The passionflower became the state flower in 1919. It was replaced by the iris in 1933. In 1973, the Tennessee government made the iris the state **cultivated** flower. The passionflower became the state wildflower.

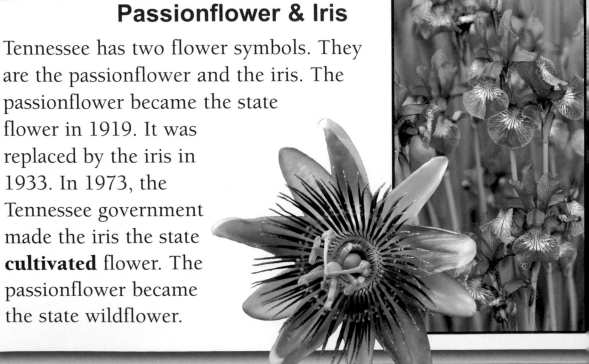

Texas
Bluebonnet

The Texas state flower is the bluebonnet. It was chosen in 1901. While bluebonnets are often blue, they can be white, lavender, pink, or red. Texas bluebonnets are blue with a white tip.

Virginia
American Dogwood

The American dogwood is the state flower of Virginia. It was chosen in 1918. American dogwood trees grow in all parts of Virginia. They are **deciduous**.

West Virginia
Rhododendron Maximum

Rhododendron maximum is a type of evergreen plant. Its flowers can be pale pink or white. They often have yellow or red specks. Rhododendron maximum became West Virginia's official flower in 1903.

The Northeast

The Northeast is the smallest region in the United States. It is east of the Great Lakes and south of Canada. The Atlantic Ocean borders the Northeast coast. There are nine states in the Northeast. They are Connecticut, Maine, Massachusetts, New Hampshire, New Jersey, New York, Pennsylvania, Rhode Island, and Vermont.

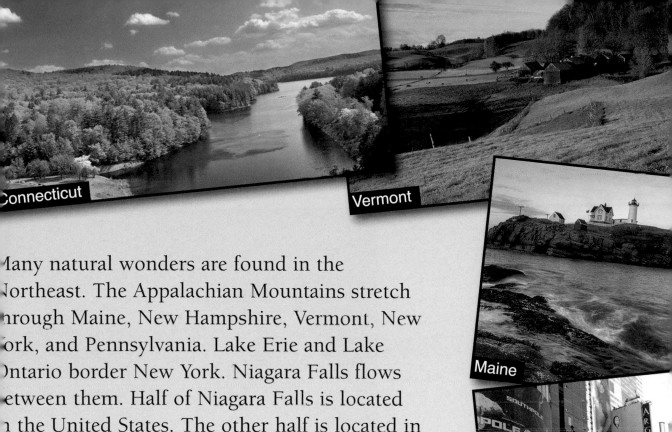
Connecticut

Vermont

Maine

Many natural wonders are found in the
Northeast. The Appalachian Mountains stretch
through Maine, New Hampshire, Vermont, New
York, and Pennsylvania. Lake Erie and Lake
Ontario border New York. Niagara Falls flows
between them. Half of Niagara Falls is located
in the United States. The other half is located in
Canada. On the U.S. side, the falls are 1,000 feet
wide and 167 feet tall.

In the 1600s, the first settlers from Europe came
to the area known as **New England**. Today, 55
million people live in the Northeast. More Irish
Americans and Italian Americans live here than
in any other part of the country. More than eight
million people live in New York City,
the largest city in the country.

New York

Web Crawler

Learn more about New England at
www.discovernewengland.org.

See spectacular views of Niagara Falls at
**www.niagarafallsstatepark.com/Destination_
PhotoGallery.aspx.**

Pennsylvania

Connecticut
Mountain Laurel

Connecticut's state flower is the mountain laurel. It was chosen in 1907. The mountain laurel is an evergreen shrub.

It grows in rocky places throughout the Northeast. Mountain laurel flowers are shaped like stars. They grow in clusters and can be rosy, pink, or white.

Maine
Eastern White Pine Cone and Tassel

Maine is the only state with an official flower that is not a flower. In 1895, Maine adopted the Eastern white pine cone and tassel as its state flower. Pine trees have cones instead of flowers. Like flowers, cones make seeds. Eastern white pine cones are 4 to 8 inches long and have smooth scales. The tassels are made of blue-green or silver-green needles.

Massachusetts
Mayflower

The mayflower became Massachusetts' state flower in 1918. It was chosen by Massachusetts' schoolchildren. The mayflower has hairy evergreen leaves and delicate blossoms. The blossoms can be pink or white. Mayflowers are known for their pleasing smell.

New Hampshire
Purple Lilac & Pink Lady's Slipper

The purple lilac became New Hampshire's state flower in 1919. This shrub has light purple flowers and heart-shaped leaves. Purple lilacs come from Europe and Asia. They were first brought to New Hampshire in 1750. New Hampshire also has a state wildflower. It is a type of orchid called the pink lady's slipper. It was chosen in 1991.

New Jersey
Common Meadow Violet

New Jersey was one of the last states to adopt an official flower. The common meadow violet became New Jersey's state flower in 1972. This wildflower grows in meadows and woodlands, and along streambanks. The meadow violet has five petals. They are a blue-purple color with a pale yellow center.

New York
Rose

In 1890, New York's schoolchildren voted the rose as the state flower. The state government officially accepted the rose in 1955. There are more than 150 species of roses in the world. A tea rose is most often used as New York's flower. Tea roses are large and have a spicy, tea-like smell.

Pennsylvania
Mountain Laurel

Like Connecticut, Pennsylvania's state flower is the mountain laurel. It was chosen in 1933. The mountain laurel is a type of **heath** plant. It is related to the huckleberry, the blueberry, and the rhododendron.

Rhode Island
Blue Violet

Schoolchildren in Rhode Island chose the bird-foot violet as the state flower in 1897. The Rhode Island government made it official in 1968. In 2001, the government changed the bird-foot violet to the blue violet.

Vermont
Red Clover

Red clover became Vermont's state flower in 1894. Red clover blooms in clusters of 100 to 125 tiny flowers. They are usually red or pink. Red clover can be eaten, and it is often used in medicines.

The National Floral Emblem

National emblems are symbols that are used for the entire country. The American flag, known as the star-spangled banner, is one such symbol. Another is the bald eagle, which is the the national bird. The oak tree is the national tree. The official flower of the United States is the rose.

President Ronald Reagan made the rose the national floral emblem on November 20, 1986.

Roses grow on thorny bushes or vines. They have soft, oval petals that are often red, pink, white, or yellow.

There are more than 150 species of roses. They are enjoyed around the world for their beauty and their sweet smell.

History of the Rose

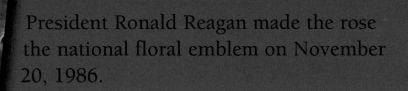

Roses have a special history in the United States. Wild roses have grown here for millions of years. In the 1500s, early settlers brought European roses to the United States. They soon became popular garden flowers. Today, roses grow in all 50 U.S. states. A rose garden borders the oval office at the White House in Washington, DC.

Guide to State Flowers

THE NATIONAL FLORAL EMBLEM
rose

ALABAMA
camellia;
oak-leaf
hydrangea

ALASKA
forget-me-not

ARIZONA
saguaro cactus
blossom

ARKANSAS
apple blossom

CALIFORNIA
golden poppy

COLORADO
white and
lavender
columbine

CONNECTICUT
mountain
laurel

DELAWARE
peach blossom

FLORIDA
orange
blossom;
tickseed

GEORGIA
Cherokee rose;
azalea

HAWAI'I
yellow hibiscus

IDAHO
syringa

ILLINOIS
blue violet

INDIANA
peony

IOWA
wild rose

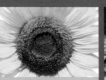

KANSAS
sunflower

KENTUCKY
goldenrod

LOUISIANA
magnolia;
Louisiana iris

MAINE
eastern white
pine cone and
tassel

MARYLAND
black-eyed
susan

MASSACHUSETTS
mayflower

MICHIGAN
apple blossom;
dwarf lake iris

MINNESOTA
pink and white
lady's slipper

MISSISSIPPI
magnolia

MISSOURI
hawthorn
blossom

MONTANA
bitterroot

NEBRASKA
goldenrod

NEVADA
sagebrush

**NEW
HAMPSHIRE**
purple lilac; pink
lady's slipper

NEW JERSEY
common
meadow violet

NEW MEXICO
yucca

NEW YORK
rose

**NORTH
CAROLINA**
dogwood
blossom

NORTH DAKOTA
wild prairie rose

OHIO
scarlet
carnation; large
white trillium

OKLAHOMA
mistletoe;
Indian blanket;
Oklahoma rose

OREGON
Oregon grape

PENNSYLVANIA
mountain
laurel

RHODE ISLAND
blue violet

SOUTH CAROLINA
yellow
jessamine; tall
goldenrod

SOUTH DAKOTA
pasque flower

TENNESSEE
passionflower;
iris

TEXAS
bluebonnet

UTAH
sego lily

VERMONT
red clover

VIRGINIA
American
dogwood

WASHINGTON
coast
rhododendron

WEST VIRGINIA
rhododendron
maximum

WISCONSIN
wood violet

WYOMING
Indian
paintbrush

Parts of a Flower

A flower is part of a plant. Most of Earth's plants have flowers. Flowers make seeds so that new plants can grow. Flowers come in many different sizes, shapes, and colors. Still, they all share the same basic traits.

STEM The stem holds the flower up. It also moves water, food, and minerals through the plant.

PETAL Petals are the main parts of a flower. They come in many shapes and are often brightly colored. Petals contain oils that give a flower its scent. This helps attract birds and insects to the flower. By brushing against the flower's center, these animals help move pollen from the stamens to the pistil, which makes seeds.

PISTIL The pistil is the female part of a flower. It grows at the very center of the flower. The pistil makes seeds with help from the stamens.

STAMEN Stamens are the male parts of a flower. They grow in a ring around the pistil. Stamens make pollen. A seed grows when pollen from a different flower contacts the pistil.

SEPAL Sepals are small, leaf-like parts below the petals. Sepals protect the flower as it grows. Most sepals are green. Others are colorful and are sometimes mistaken for petals. The Indian paintbrush, for example, is a flower with very colorful sepals. Some flowers, such as tulips, have no sepals at all.

Test Your Knowledge

1 List the nine states with more than one flower symbol.

4 Read the flowers below. Which one is not a state flower of a western state?
- a. white and lavender columbine
- b. syringa
- c. mayflower
- d. forget-me-not
- e. sagebrush

2 Name the five states that have a type of rose as their state flower or wildflower.

5 How many states have a type of blue violet as their state flower?

3 Which four states have chosen the blossoms of fruit trees as their state flowers?

6 What is the state flower of both Connecticut and Pennsylvania?

7 Read the choices below. Which two southern states do not share the same state flower or wildflower?
- a. Louisiana and Mississippi
- b. North Carolina and Virginia
- c. Kentucky and South Carolina
- d. Maryland and West Virginia

8 Other than blue, what colors can the bluebonnet be?

9

Read the choices below. Which Midwest state has a flower that only grows in gardens?
- a. South Dakota's pasque flower
- b. Iowa's wild rose
- c. Missouri's hawthorn blossom
- d. Nebraska's goldenrod
- e. Indiana's peony

13

Which state flower is often used in medicines?

10

What is the Spanish name for California's golden poppy?

14

How have people in the West used the roots of bitterroot, yucca, and sego lily plants?

11

Read the choices below. Which state flower of the West has colorful sepals that are often mistaken for petals?
- a. saguaro cactus blossom
- b. Indian paintbrush
- c. Oregon grape
- d. coast rhododendron
- e. yellow hibiscus

15

Which state flower is not really a flower?

12

Which state is called the "sunflower state"?

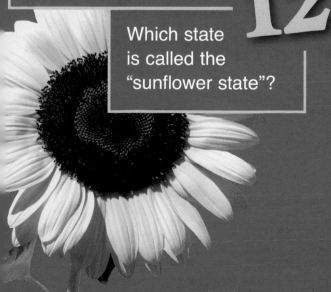

Answers:

1. Ohio, Alabama, Florida, Georgia, Louisiana, Oklahoma, South Carolina, Tennessee, New Hampshire 2. Iowa – wild rose; North Dakota – wild prairie rose; Georgia – Cherokee rose; Oklahoma – Oklahoma rose; New York – rose 3. Arkansas – apple; Michigan – apple; Florida – orange; Delaware – peach 4. c. Mayflower – Massachusetts 5. Four – Illinois, New Jersey, Rhode Island, and Wisconsin 6. mountain laurel 7. d. Maryland and West Virginia 8. blue, white, lavender, pink, or red 9. Indiana's peony 10. copa de oro, "cup of gold." 11. b. Indian paintbrush 12. Kansas 13. red clover 14. Montana – for food; New Mexico – for soap; Utah – for food 15. Maine's eastern white pine cone and tassel

U.S. Sites and Symbols (45)

Create Your Own Floral Emblem

Create a flower symbol to represent your community or school. Begin by thinking about what type of flower you want. Use this book to help you. What kinds of flowers grow in the region where you live? Will your flower grow in the ground, on a shrub, or on a tree?

Think about how your flower will look. Will your flower be large or small? How many petals will each blossom have? What colors will your flower be? Why? Look at the pictures in this book for help. You can also view thousands of plant and flower images online at the Ladybird Johnson Wildflower Center **www.wildflower.org/gallery**.

Draw your flower on a piece of paper. Use the diagram on pages 42 and 43 to help you design the parts of your flower. Color your drawing with felt markers or crayons. When you are finished, label the parts of your flower.

Write a description of your flower. What kind of flower is it? Where does it grow? What does it say about you?

Further Research

Many books and websites provide information on state flowers. To learn more about flowers, borrow books from the library, or surf the Internet.

Books

Most libraries have computers that connect to a database for researching information. If you input a key word, you will be provided with a list of books in the library that contain information on that topic. Non-fiction books are arranged numerically, using their call number. Fiction books are organized alphabetically by the author's last name.

Websites

Find fun facts about each of the 50 U.S. states by clicking on this map from the U.S. Census Bureau: **www.census.gov/schools/facts**.

Learn more about flowers, their uses, and meanings at **www.familymanagement.com/holidays/flowers/index.html**.

Read about the different parts of a flower at **www.enchantedlearning.com/subjects/plants/printouts/ floweranatomy.shtml**. Click on the highlighted terms to find out more about them.

Make fun flower crafts using the instructions at **www.enchantedlearning.com/crafts/flowers**.

Glossary

citizenship: being a citizen of a city or country

cultivated: land that has been prepared to use for growing

deciduous: plants or trees that drop their leaves every year

endangered: the threat of becoming extinct

evergreen: plants or trees that have green leaves or needles all year long

Great Plains: a vast grassland region covering 10 U.S. states and 4 Canadian provinces. Used for farming and raising cattle

heath: flat, open land covered with low bushes

herb: a plant used for flavoring food during cooking or for medicine

New England: a region of the United States made up of Maine, Vermont, New Hampshire, Massachusetts, Rhode Island, and Connecticut

ray flowers: flowers in the daisy family with long flat petals that grow on the outer edge of the head of a plant

sepals: parts of plants, shaped like leaves, that lie at the base of a flower

Index